Editor-in-Chief and Founder:
  Lyndon H. LaRouche, Jr.
Editorial Board: *Lyndon H. LaRouche, Jr. , Helga
  Zepp-LaRouche, Robert Ingraham, Tony
  Papert, Gerald Rose, Dennis Small, Jeffrey
  Steinberg, William Wertz*
Co-Editors: *Robert Ingraham, Tony Papert*
Managing Editor: *Nancy Spannaus*
Technology: *Marsha Freeman*
Books: *Katherine Notley*
Ebooks: *Richard Burden*
Graphics: *Alan Yue*
Photos: *Stuart Lewis*
Circulation Manager: *Stanley Ezrol*

INTELLIGENCE DIRECTORS
Counterintelligence: *Jeffrey Steinberg, Michele
  Steinberg*
Economics: *John Hoefle, Marcia Merry Baker,
  Paul Gallagher*
History: *Anton Chaitkin*
Ibero-America: *Dennis Small*
Russia and Eastern Europe: *Rachel Douglas*
United States: *Debra Freeman*

INTERNATIONAL BUREAUS
Bogotá: *Miriam Redondo*
Berlin: *Rainer Apel*
Copenhagen: *Tom Gillesberg*
Houston: *Harley Schlanger*
Lima: *Sara Madueño*
Melbourne: *Robert Barwick*
Mexico City: *Gerardo Castilleja Chávez*
New Delhi: *Ramtanu Maitra*
Paris: *Christine Bierre*
Stockholm: *Ulf Sandmark*
United Nations, N.Y.C.: *Leni Rubinstein*
Washington, D.C.: *William Jones*
Wiesbaden: *Göran Haglund*

ON THE WEB
e-mail: eirns@larouchepub.com
www.larouchepub.com
www.executiveintelligencereview.com
www.larouchepub.com/eiw
Webmaster: *John Sigerson*
Assistant Webmaster: *George Hollis*
Editor, Arabic-language edition: *Hussein Askary*

EIR (ISSN 0273-6314) *is published weekly
(50 issues), by EIR News Service, Inc.,
P.O. Box 17390, Washington, D.C. 20041-0390.
(703) 777-9451 ext. 415*

European Headquarters: E.I.R. GmbH, Postfach
Bahnstrasse 9a, D-65205, Wiesbaden, Germany
Tel: 49-611-73650
Homepage: http://www.eirna.com
e-mail: eirna@eirna.com
Director: Georg Neudecker

Montreal, Canada: 514-461-1557

Denmark: EIR - Danmark, Sankt Knuds Vej 11,
basement left, DK-1903 Frederiksberg, Denmark.
Tel.: +45 35 43 60 40, Fax: +45 35 43 87 57. e-mail:
eirdk@hotmail.com.

Mexico City: EIR, Sor Juana Inés de la Cruz 242-2
Col. Agricultura C.P. 11360
Delegación M. Hidalgo, México D.F.
Tel. (5525) 5318-2301
eirmexico@gmail.com

Impeach Obama
As a British Puppet

EIR Contents

www.larouchepub.com Volume 43, Number 40, September 30, 2016

Cover This Week

Obama, the marionette

CC/Rvaldez4108

LAROUCHE PAC WEBCAST

Obama's Veto of JASTA Must Be Crushed Now!

It is reprehensible that one man is standing between justice for the murder of 3,000 people and this legislation becoming law.

—Kristen Breitweiser
9/11 widow

Sept. 24—On Friday afternoon, September 23, 2016, President Barack Obama vetoed the Justice Against Sponsors of Terrorism Act (JASTA), legislation which had been passed unanimously by both the United States Senate and the House of Representatives. As this issue of EIR goes to press, an intensive mobilization to override the President's veto is being carried out by LaRouche PAC, the survivors and victims of the 9/11 attacks, first-responders to those attacks, and many, many other concerned and patriotic Americans. The moment of truth has arrived as to whether justice will be given to the victims of 9/11 and whether those who were responsible will be held accountable.

More than seven years ago, on April 11, 2009, Lyndon LaRouche delivered a live historic webcast in which he diagnosed the mental unfitness of Barack Obama to hold the office of the Presidency. Mr. LaRouche presented a clinical profile of Obama's murderous narcissistic personality. Dismissed by many at the time, the validity of that warning by Mr. LaRouche has now been proven.

By the time this article appears, the question of a potential override of Obama's veto of JASTA may well have been settled, but regardless of the outcome, the

urgency for the immediate removal of Obama from office will remain. We print here edited excerpts from the LaRouche PAC International Webcast of Sept. 23, 2016 that deal with these matters.

Matthew Ogden: Good afternoon! It's September 23rd, 2016. My name is Matthew Ogden, and I would like to welcome all of you to

LPAC TV

Background: Pro-JASTA organizers. Foreground, participants in Sept. 23 LPAC webcast, top to bottom: Matthew Ogden, moderator; Elliot Greenspan, from New York; Jeffrey Steinberg, EIR.

a special broadcast here from LaRouchepac.com on Friday afternoon. We are broadcasting our regularly scheduled webcast *early* this week at 4:00 Eastern Time because we are in the midst of a showdown in Washington, D.C., where every minute counts.

I'm joined in the studio by Jeff Steinberg, from *Executive Intelligence Review,* and we're joined via video by Elliot Greenspan, coordinator for LaRouche PAC activities in New York City.

All-Out Battle Behind the Scenes

As all of you know, we're in the countdown to the "moment of truth" right now. As of 1:00-2:00 this afternoon, during the White House press briefing, it remains clear that President Obama is committed to vetoing the JASTA Bill (Senate Bill 2040). We're going to put, right now, the phone number on the screen for you to call in to Congress in order to contact the Senators and Representatives from your State, in order for you to be mobilized *during the show.* Don't even delay. Call in. Make sure that your voice is heard. Tell every single Member of Congress to remain strong in their commitment to override Obama's veto. [Capitol Switchboard: 202 224-3131]

This Justice Against Sponsors of Terrorism Act (or JASTA), despite unbelievable pressure, threats, lies, money, and intimidation coming from the Saudi lobbying machine and from the White House directly,— at last reading on Capitol Hill, Congress is still set to override this veto, delivering a very historic first veto override of Obama's entire Presidency.

What's become clear from the coverage, is that this has been an all-out battle behind the scenes. I'd like to read just the beginning of a *New York Times* article that came out on Wednesday, September 21st, which was headlined, "Fight Between Saudis and 9/11 Families Escalates in Washington." I think this gives a dramatic overview of exactly what has gone down behind the scenes, and in public view, during the course of just the few days this week. It reads, in the beginning:

> On Monday, a constellation of lobbyists for Saudi Arabia, which has spent more than $5 million this past year to buy influence in Washington, called a crisis meeting to try to stop legislation allowing the families of victims of the Sept. 11 attacks to sue the Saudi government for any role in the plot.
>
> On Tuesday, the 9/11 families, represented in

their multibillion-dollar lawsuits by lawyers including Jack Quinn, a former White House counsel with deep relationships in Washington, demonstrated outside the White House to pressure President Obama not to veto the legislation, as he has vowed to do.

On Wednesday, these two powerful forces, one operating in the shadows and the other more in the open, converged on Capitol Hill in the culmination of one of the biggest and most emotional lobbying fights of the year. The battle is a reflection of the enduring dominance in Washington of the 9/11 families and the diminishing clout here of Saudi Arabia, which once advanced its agenda unencumbered in the West Wing and the corridors of Congress.

LaRouche's 'Marching Orders'

Now I think it's very clear that what has happened, is that the 9/11 families—but also other citizens, including those of you who are watching this broadcast here today—have played a central role in fueling this showdown. And that's why we're asking you, *right now,* if you haven't called in to your Congressmen, to call right now—202-224-3121—to say "Override Obama's threatened veto of JASTA."

We do have some video clips from the press conference that occurred on the Senate side of the Capitol on Tuesday afternoon, where Terry Strada, Kaitlyn Strada, Alison Crowther—all three members of the 9/11 families—and also Senator Richard Blumenthal (D-Conn.) absolutely demolished and debunked the lies that were coming out of the Obama Administration and the Saudi lobbying machine.

But before we get to that, I'd like to ask Jeff Steinberg to say, in brief, what Mr. LaRouche's "marching orders" for this moment are, in the face of Obama's upcoming threatened veto of the JASTA Bill. And then we will play this press conference clip. Jeff, I'm going to let you just summarize what Mr. LaRouche's comments were today.

Jeff Steinberg: It's pretty straightforward. He just simply said that if Obama goes ahead with this veto, then he should be immediately impeached. This is such an act of overt and witting treason against not just the 9/11 families, but against the United States as a whole.

One of the news accounts today said that if Obama goes ahead with his veto, then once again he's siding

LPAC/Jason Ross

Terry Strada of 9/11 Families & Survivors United for Justice Against Terrorism, as she addressed the Sept. 20, 2016 press conference at the U.S. Senate in support of JASTA.

with the terrorists, against the interests of the United States.

In the Preamble to the U.S. Constitution, one of the first responsibilities of the President is to defend the national security of the United States: to "provide for the common defense" and to "promote the general Welfare," and if President Obama cannot see why it is in the urgent interests of all Americans, and of anyone around the world who wants to actually fight against this terrorist scourge emanating from Saudi Wahhabism and from the Saudi Royal Family,— then he had better think about what the implications of this are.

Mr. LaRouche's marching orders are very simple: Get the veto override. Mobilize your Senator, mobilize your Representative. But, on top of that, anyone who is unclear about the strategic implications of an Obama veto, should think long and hard and should join in the chorus that must immediately demand his impeachment from office. This is a deadly serious matter, and that's the step that must be taken.

9/11 Families Speak

Ogden: Great! We're going to elaborate a little bit more on the context of that a little bit later. But right now, I want to play a very short excerpt from the speeches of Terry Strada, Kaitlyn Strada, Alison Crowther, and Sen. Blumenthal, in which they debunk every single media propaganda line that you're going to

hear coming from the White House and the Saudi lobbying machine on the subject of the JASTA Bill. Here is that excerpt:

Terry Strada: In our quest for the truth, accountability, and justice for the murder of my husband and the thousands of other innocent souls lost and injured, my colleagues and I have worked tirelessly with Congress for over four years, advocating for the 9/11 families in support of the Justice Against Sponsors of Terrorism Act (JASTA).

I am frustrated, angry, and tired of the mis-truths being carelessly spewed about this legislation, and I am here today to set the record straight. The President's rationales to veto JASTA hold no weight. They are 100% wrong. The issues the White House is raising now ... have all been considered, repeatedly, and addressed.

This issue about the possibility of threats of reciprocal laws and lawsuits is a knee-jerk reaction, raised by all novices looking at the Bill, until they actually read the text and consider the policies. Then, only those who would favor Saudi interests seem to cling to the mistruths. Those who favor sound, anti-terror-financing policies, support JASTA.

The most recent statement from the White House Press Secretary, Josh Earnest, last Monday, when he told the White House press corps that there were concerns about judges all over the country designating terror organizations for U.S. sanctions, is nonsensical. No judge overseeing a civil jury trial for injuries would ever be imposing U.S. sanctions. That is simply outlandish.

'Denying Us Justice Is Un-American'

To be crystal clear: JASTA does not and cannot have anything to do with suing our diplomats. That issue is controlled by something entirely different from JASTA—the Vienna Convention on Diplomatic Relations. And if *I* know it, I suspect the White House knows this, too.

JASTA has nothing to do with whether a private citizen, or even a private company, can be sued for alleged wrong-doing. JASTA deals with the immunity of foreign states. So, the White House's press comments that enacting JASTA will threaten suits against the United States—which Mr. Earnest emphasized as a risk of

LPAC/Jason Ross

Sen. Richart Blumenthal (D-Conn.): "If the Saudi Government is innocent, it has nothing to fear."

JASTA—are categorically untrue. I am sure the White House knows that, too.

And most importantly, our military is not at risk for being sued if JASTA is enacted. The narrow text of JASTA, like our legal history, specifically distinguishes between acts of war and acts of terrorism. The text of the Bill, for anyone who cares to read it—and it is surprisingly short—specifically excludes acts of war. I'm sure the White House knows that, too.

No one who seriously opposes terrorism disagrees with a bill that at its core, accuses no one. All JASTA does, is simply ask those accused of sponsoring terrorist attacks on U.S. soil, to answer on the merits and to stand to account for those accusations.

For us, the 9/11 families and survivors, all we're asking for is an opportunity to have our case heard in a courtroom. Denying us justice is un-American. In our case, the existing and still growing mountain of evidence against the Kingdom of Saudi Arabia, demands that they address those accusations, if for nothing else, to normalize our relations with a nation that claims to be our ally.

I would suggest, that if the Kingdom had no part in the horrific attacks of 9/11, they should welcome the opportunity to address the allegations head-on, and fix our relationship. Instead, they have hired dozens of highly paid lobbyists, who roam the halls of Congress,

intimidating our Members of Congress and trying to strong-arm our legislative process. This, too, is un-American.

We, the 9/11 community, have suffered far too long at the hands of far too many that would prevent us from seeking accountability before a jury of our peers. Neither the President, nor Congress, nor the lobbyists for foreign kingdoms should be permitted to make us wait another day to pass JASTA.

Saudis 'Should Be Held Accountable'

Sen. Richard Blumenthal: The basic objective here is to hold accountable wrong-doers and law-breakers and evil-doers. Because that is the rule of law. Behind that over-arching, seemingly abstract ideal, is a loop-hole in the law. And it's a modest loop-hole. The loop-hole is that a foreign actor or agent can commit an atrocity in this country, but be immune from any kind of legal accountability if the aiding and abetting is done outside our boundaries. That's basically what may well be shown in a court of law about the Saudi agents or operatives who aided and abetted the 9/11 terrorists. There's a basic principle here. If a foreign agent or actor gives a bag of money or a ton of explosives to someone who then does harm in our country, and it happens outside the country, there still should be legal accountability ...

Take an analogy: If another country launched a missile from within its borders, from its soil, that blew up an American citizen, nobody would say, "Well, that's okay, because they did it within their own borders." And the same principle applies here. A foreign government that aids and abets an act of terror that does harm in our country, should be held accountable, even if those actions occurred outside our borders ...

If the Saudi Government is innocent, it has nothing to fear from a day in court. If it is culpable, it should be held accountable. And there is mounting evidence, revealed in the 28 pages, kept secret for so long, about potential Saudi complicity.

So, I am urging the President, as I did in a letter with my colleague Sen. Chuck Schumer (D-N.Y.) about ten days ago, to sign this measure, and I believe that there are now, and there will be, well more than the necessary

LPAC/Jason Ross

Kaitlyn Strada: "Show that you, our elected officials, stand on our side, that of the American citizens."

LPAC/Jason Ross

Alison Crowther: "We are engaged in an insidious war of hearts and minds."

votes to override this veto. It was unanimously passed, and I believe it will be overwhelmingly approved again, if need be.

'Do Not Yield to Powerful Influences'

Kaitlyn Strada: After hearing our cries for justice, our U.S. Senate and House of Representatives unanimously passed legislation called the Justice Against Sponsors of Terrorism Act. This bill would give me and thousands of other children who lost their parents on 9/11, the opportunity to see some degree of accountability. JASTA does not determine whether the accused foreign state is actually responsible; the accused just wouldn't get a free pass on accountability. Under existing law, a foreign state alleged to be responsible for a car wreck has no free pass and must face the music; the same should be true for terrorist attacks that kill or cause injury to Americans on U.S. soil. It is the right thing.

So, I am imploring Congress to override the President's impending veto, and help my family and all the 9/11 families and survivors seek the justice we deserve. Fifteen years is far too long for us to have to wait already. The veto should be overridden at the first opportunity, and we should not be forced to wait a day longer. Please show that you, our elected officials, stand on *our* side, that of the American citizens. Do not yield to the pressure of powerful foreign influences looking to escape accountability. It's past time to enact JASTA.

'An Epic Battle for the Soul of Humanity'

Alison Crowther: I've come here today along with many other 9/11 families and victims in support of the Justice Against Sponsors of Terrorism Act. The purpose of this act is to hold accountable individuals in nations that fund terrorist activities in our country. JASTA, if passed, will open pathways to choke off foreign sources of funding and bankrupt terrorism. We first and foremost exhort President Obama to approve JASTA. We are engaged in an insidious war of hearts and minds, an epic battle for the soul of humanity. To quote President Franklin Delano Roosevelt, "The only thing we have to fear, is fear itself." If we allow fear of potential consequences to rule over right action, the bad guys will win.

JASTA is a weapon in our nonviolent arsenal to fight against those who would intentionally target and perpetrate heinous crimes against innocent men, women, children, and the unborn. If President Obama decides to veto JASTA, we trust that the Senate and House, who represent the will of the 9/11 families and the citizens of our great country, will stand by their unanimous convictions and override a Presidential veto of JASTA without delay. Thank you very much.

Ogden: Now while you were watching that video, we received a breaking news announcement; I am going to let Jeff announce to you what has just developed.

Now the Onus Is on You

Steinberg: At 4:27 this afternoon, President Obama signed the veto of JASTA.

This now means that the onus is on all of you and on the members of the U.S. Senate and then the U.S. House of Representatives to deliver a unanimous rebuke to a President who puts his future business dealings with Saudi Arabia and his commitment to cover up the crimes of 9/11, ahead of the interests of the American people. This is a *shameful moment* for the institution of the Presidency; and I hope all of you will take that absolutely seriously and do your part as citizens. As Mr. LaRouche said, "This is an unconscionable act by President Obama that deserves his immediate impeachment." But first and foremost, he's got to be delivered a brutal message by the Congress, by the Senate; but first by you, the American people, that this is thoroughly unacceptable. He will go down in infamy for this hideous act on his part.

I just want to amplify a little bit what the stakes are in this fight. We all know that 2,997 people perished on 9/11; but the death and destruction from that event continues to this day. I want to read to you a news item that I wrote earlier this afternoon, and I think you'll understand why this is an appropriate thing to be reading to you right now:

On the weekend of the 15th anniversary of the September 11, 2001 attacks earlier this month, *Newsweek* magazine published an extensive report on the tens of thousands of New Yorkers and other first responders who are suffering severe medical conditions as the result of their heroics following the 9/11 attacks. The *Newsweek* story was graphically headlined, "9/11's Second Wave: Cancer and Other Diseases Linked to the 2001 Attacks Are Surging." While much of the article was devoted to heartbreaking case studies of the first responders who are now either dead or are suffering serious illnesses as the result of their efforts, the statistics provided in the article are harrowing, and reveal the extent to which the consequences of the 9/11 attacks continue to take lives.

The Body Count Is Continuing

This is a quote from *Newsweek:* "Doctors with the World Trade Center Health Program, which the federal government created in the aftermath of the attacks, have linked nearly 70 types of cancer to Ground Zero. Many people have fallen victim to cancers their doctors say are rare, aggressive, and particularly hard to treat."

More than 411 emergency rescue workers died in the immediate aftermath of the 9/11 attack on the World Trade Center, and that number has reached 1,064 as of July 2016, according to data that *Newsweek* obtained from the Centers for Disease Control and Prevention and the Occupational Safety and Health Administration (OSHA). But the full account is staggering: "As many as 400,000 people are estimated to be affected by diseases such as cancers and mental illnesses linked to September 11th." Four hundred thousand! That figure includes those who lived and worked within a mile and a half of Ground Zero in Manhattan and Brooklyn, the vast majority of whom still don't know they're at risk. Mark Farfel, director of the World Trade Center Health Registry, which tracks the health of more than 71,000 rescue workers and survivors, says, "Many people don't connect the symptoms they have today to September 11th."

Dr. Michael Crane, director of a clinic at Mount Sinai Hospital which treats 22,000 rescue and recovery workers from 9/11, told *Newsweek:* "Today, fifteen years after the attacks, doctors are starting to understand why people are still dying. When the towers came down, they released a massive plume of carcinogens, turning lower Manhattan into a cesspool of cancer and deadly disease."

A Natural Resources Defense Council report, issued soon after the 9/11 attacks, estimated that the North Tower alone released 400 tons of asbestos into the atmosphere, along with lead, mercury, volatile organic compounds, and deadly poisons. Among New York City firefighters, the cancer rate after 9/11 increased by between 19 and 30 percent over pre-9/11 rates.

So the body count is continuing, and therefore, the magnitude of the President's crime in failing to sign JASTA into law, is that much greater.

Ogden: I am going to hand over to Elliot right now in New York City. The activity on the ground is intense, both in terms of forcing an override on this JASTA veto, but also activity for ushering in a New Paradigm, a new international economic order, which is now on the table for discussion at the United Nations General Assembly meeting. I'm going to let Elliot say a little more about the situation there.

Report from Manhattan

Elliot Greenspan: Thank you, Matt. Four concerts—this is now two weeks ago—four concerts were performed as a living memorial to the 3,000 who perished on 9/11, to the first responders, to the survivors, to

Chinese TV

The Sept. 4-5 G-20 Summit in Hangzhou, China, led by President of China Xi Jinping, concentrated on creating a new financial architecture committed to a new economic order.

the families, and to the millions of victims in regime-change wars caused by the Bush and Obama administrations. A living memorial. We had upwards of 3,000 New Yorkers at these concerts; we had reached at least 100,000, probably hundreds of thousands of New Yorkers in the run-up to this, for the purpose of focussing the city, the metropolitan area, and the nation, on 9/11, on the implication of the declassification of the 28 pages, and on the potential for a breakthrough with JASTA. So this goes back a couple of weeks. Then, we come to the UN General Assembly.

Among other events at the General Assembly, is the intervention by the Saudi government spokesman before the General Assembly—that is, before the world— saying that JASTA was an affront to the sovereignty of Saudi Arabia. At the same time, the *Wall Street Journal* in New York is editorializing against JASTA; the *New York Post* has a Congressional op-ed supporting JASTA; and there were two major *New York Times* articles in the last two days. This situation is super-charged.

In that context, we released—twice this week—editions five and six of the LaRouche newspaper, the *Hamiltonian,* which had headlines, "Traitor Obama Stalls on JASTA, Impeachment is Nigh," and "Obama's Doomsday: First JASTA, Next Glass-Steagall." Insofar as Obama has perpetuated the Bush-Cheney policy, the British-Saudi policy of regime-change war and of international terrorism, we took the gloves off in Manhattan over these last days, targeting Obama. We had banners

at our rallies throughout especially the East Side near the United Nations, Midtown, and the Upper West Side: "LaRouche: Cameron Is Out; Make Obama Next!" and "Good-bye Cameron: Take the Pig with You," which had a picture of a pig with Obama's face on the pig. Also, "Duterte Was Right! Obama is a Son-of-a-B****," "Obama's Legacy—5 Wars, 60 Million Refugees," "Obama Backs ISIS in Syria," and it goes on like this. We hammered away at this.

A Transformation Is Building

Let me, however, locate this in the broader context of the UN General Assembly. There was a revolution to finish off the British Empire on the 4th and 5th of September at the Hangzhou summit of the Group of 20 (G-20), led by the Chinese under the direction of President Xi Jinping. There was the creation of a new financial architecture, and of an international governance agency—the G-20—which is committed to a new economic order, the New Silk Road, and the World Land-Bridge,— ideas which were put forward in 1975 by Lyndon LaRouche, and which were brought by LaRouche's allies, in particular Guyana's Foreign Minister Fred Wills, to the United Nations General Assembly for the first time 40 years ago this week.

Without going through that history, those ideas, which we've organized for, day by day for over 40 years, have now created a new economic system based on scientific and technological progress and great projects of infrastructure. This occurs at a moment when Deutsche Bank, the Italian banks, and the London and Wall Street banks are facing their demise—far beyond the 2008 explosion.

In that context, we see the creation of this new system. The Chinese government, under Premier Li Keqiang, over the last several days, has brought this breakthrough, the commitment of the G-20 summit, to the United Nations General Assembly. He has put forward the conception of the UN Sustainable Development 2030 Agenda, which is a commitment adopted a year ago by the UN General Assembly to eliminate poverty by the year 2030. What the Chinese have done, is to emphasize the "development" part of "sustainable development," and they've enlisted the United Nations Development Program (UNDP) in a first Memorandum of Understanding between the UNDP and the Chinese government.

swiss-image.ch/Michael Buholzer

China's Premier Li Keqiang brought to the UN General Assembly the commitment of the G-20 summit to development, while Obama convened a summit at the UN on the refugee crisis, which his policies have created. Here Li Keqiang speaks at the World Economic Forum in Davos, Switzerland, Jan. 21, 2015.

There is a transformation building, as a result of the leadership of President Xi with President Putin and with the BRICS nations as a unit, which has become ever stronger through several summits—the G-20 of early September, into the General Assembly, and from here into the BRICS summit in mid-October in India. A new economic potential is unfolding for humanity. The Chinese have standing on the matter. As President Xi put it at Hangzhou, they have eliminated poverty for 700 million Chinese; they will eliminate poverty for 57 million more by 2020. They're spreading this through the New Silk Road already to at least 70 nations, and soon 100.

Intervening into a Super-Charged Environment

The great question is, what is the United States doing in response? What is Western Europe doing? In a discussion with Mr. and Mrs. LaRouche this morning, Mrs. LaRouche emphasized that China is the stellar nation fighting for this perspective; but no such thing is coming from the United States or from Western Europe yet, and instead, one sees the treason of Obama in his aiding and abetting of ISIS, al-Qaeda, and al-Nusra's international terrorism. What an irony that Obama convened a summit on the refugee crisis at the UN this week! Obama created the refugee crisis!

So in our work on the streets of Manhattan this week, there was a super-charged environment. There was a battleground there. There was, for example, a demonstration heavily funded by George Soros and the neocons attacking the Presidency of Rouhani of Iran—about 500 demonstrators attacking Rouhani. Joe Lieberman became the spokesman of that demonstration, and Joe Lieberman announced that it's Iran that is responsible—he says—for the mass murder of Syrians. Daniel Burke, LaRouche PAC leading organizer in the city, happened upon this demonstration and he yelled out, "Lieberman, you're lying! Obama and the Saudis are responsible for the mass murder in Syria!" There was a brief dialogue, and Lieberman at some point seemed to agree with Daniel Burke.

Then there was a demonstration organized by the Syrian-American Forum, including large numbers of Syrian-Americans and others, and Lynne Speed—leading LaRouche organizer in New York—took the microphone and outlined what we have done to create the potential for this transformation in Syria. One of the Syrians there asked, "What about Senator Richard Black?" And Lynne answered, "Yes, he just spoke at a Schiller Institute conference which was addressed by Jeff Steinberg, by Helga LaRouche, by Ambassador Ja'afari of Syria." And Lynne developed the potential to end this regime-change policy by virtue of the G-20 agenda, of the Chinese and Russian agenda. To crush terrorism militarily, and to develop and reconstruct that region.

Daniel was interviewed at the same time by ABC Television in New York, and was asked, "Well, President Obama is giving his final UN address. What do you anticipate?" And Daniel said, "It's going to be treason; it's going to be a disaster. Obama has created the refugee crisis," and he spelled out the alternative policy which is what we now have on the table.

'If More Americans Were Like You ...'

Let me conclude: The new *Hamiltonian*—and I should emphasize that the lead report in the *Hamiltonian* and the banner headline is: "Appeal to the UN General Assembly: A New Paradigm for the Common Aims of Mankind." Helga Zepp-LaRouche penned this appeal explicitly to build upon the G-20 breakthrough, the G-20 revolution, and that was the challenge that she posed to the governments of the world, many of whom are receiving this *Hamiltonian*; we've gotten out about 4,000 *Hamiltonians* in several days. We will intensify this over the weekend and into next week. The idea is the challenge to the governments of the world to join

LPAC

LPAC organizers near the UN General Assembly in New York, advocating China's implementation of LaRouche's World Land-Bridge perspective as the alternative to the refugee crisis.

China and Russia and India and the BRICS; to join La-Rouche under LaRouche's leadership.

This morning, as we were distributing this and organizing, a Chinese businessman came to our table, and said, "If the United States and China work together, we can solve all the problems of the world. Drugs, terrorism, war. But the United States doesn't want to do it. India and China are doing things; in the United States, it's just talk and fighting. If you want to be rich, build a road. It makes everyone richer. If more Americans were like you," he said to our organizers, "we could solve all problems." I think that's a useful microcosm. This is the LaRouche movement, the new Presidency which La-Rouche is creating, centered in New York with the Hamiltonian—our drive to work with China and the BRICS countries. That's my report.

Ogden: Thank you very much, Elliot. As can be made no clearer, the lever of history is in our hands. Many members of the LaRouche PAC New York City chapter took the bus down to Washington, D.C. to be involved in these JASTA rallies. That made a huge difference in the White House rally and the Senate rally. These are people who have the physical means to do that. You, right now, can pick up the telephone and call

Congress. We still have a few more minutes on the East Coast before Congress leaves for the weekend. Call them now! That's why we're recording at this early time. We're going to display again the phone number on the screen. This is the Capitol switchboard; you can call both of your Senators, and you can call your member in the House of Representatives, and tell them now is the time to override Obama's veto.

Financial Collapse and Glass-Steagall

Steinberg: I want to say two things. Number one, I think for those citizens out there who've not engaged in this kind of level of political mobilization, let me be very clear. If you walk into any office on Capitol Hill, the first thing you encounter are several young people, usually they're new employees—fresh out of college—sometimes they're even interns. They're there taking phone calls. And they are instructed by every member of Congress, to take detailed notes on every constituent call that comes in there. And of course, we're two months away from elections in which every member of the House and one-third of the Senate are up for re-election. They want to know what issues are on their constituents' minds.

When Congress was considering whether to give

President Obama the authority to bomb Syria back in September of 2013, the switchboards were ringing off the hook on Capitol Hill. Every office received massive numbers of phone calls, emails, and letters; and they were running 100 to 1 against any kind of new wars in the Middle East involving the United States. So, you do make a difference.

I think the other thing that needs to be remembered in the context of what Elliot has just reported, is that one of the things that is going on, on both sides of the Atlantic, is that the entire financial system is crumbling at an accelerating rate. If anything, we are also at a moment where not only is it necessary to pass JASTA and to get this treacherous President out of office—not wait 'til January, not wait 'til the November elections—but now! After what he's just done, it should be clear as day. But the other thing that's got to be done immediately, is Congress must take up the Glass-Steagall Act. There are bills in both Houses of Congress to reinstate Glass-Steagall, which means breaking up the too-big-to-fail banks.

The FDIC, the Federal Deposit Insurance Corporation, which insures your deposits in the Federal commercial banks across the United States, has issued a report in the last few days in which it reported in great detail and with great alarm, that the major banks of Europe and the United States have once again built up such a mountain of leveraged debt that they could blow at any moment ... The leverage that these banks have built up criminally, is worse than where things stood at the time that Lehman Brothers blew out. The leverage of debt to reserves of Deutsche Bank is over 37 to 1; and all the other banks that we're talking about here have leverage ratios of 25 to 1, or 30 to 1.

So this whole system is about to blow, and once again, the Obama administration, in the same way it's opposed to JASTA, is opposed to reinstating Glass-Steagall. Congress has to really stand up, and you've got to be the spine that pushes that issue forward, as well as what we've been talking about in the first part of this show—about the urgency of a veto override of JASTA and moves to bring this President down all together.

Ogden: I could foresee Glass-Steagall being the second veto override of Obama's administration.

Steinberg: Right, exactly. And it's got to happen in September. We can't wait 'til after November for this,

LPAC

LPAC organizers near UN headquarters in New York are getting across to people the necessity of restoring FDR's Glass-Steagall Act as a precondition for rebuilding the U.S. economy and enabling the United States to play a positive role in the development of the world.

it's too risky.

New Presidency Without Hillary or Trump

Ogden: Absolutely. The appeal that Elliot referenced from Helga Zepp-LaRouche, which is now going into the hands of UN ambassadors and others as we speak, is critical. At the same time, I know that over the course of this weekend, everything will be dominated by this fight over the JASTA veto override. Congress will be in session at the beginning of next week. The district offices, high-profile appearances, op-eds, and calls into radio shows: everything that you can do over the next 24-48 hours, will determine what happens on Monday morning when Congress comes back into session.

So again, the number is on the screen—202 224-

EIRNS/Stephan Ossenkopp

Helga Zepp-LaRouche at the T-20 Summit in Beijing, China, July 29, 2016, which laid some of the groundwork for the G-20 Summit.

3121—so you can call into your Congressional office; you still have a few moments left to do so. Circulate this broadcast as widely as you can. That video excerpt that we showed you with Terry Strada, the other 9/11 families, and Senator Blumenthal is available on the La-Rouche PAC website. You can circulate that, too. That debunks all of the lies that are coming from the Obama White House and the Saudi political lobbying machine; you can use that to inform your own activism over the course of this week.

Elliot, do you have any final words from New York to conclude this show?

Greenspan: Insofar as Lyndon La-Rouche's objective with the creation of the *Hamiltonian* newspaper was to launch a new Presidency of the United States, a new institution of the Presidency independent of these hated candidates and independent of Obama,— this is a fascinating and decisive moment, in which Obama, for the first time in his entire Presidency, is about to be overidden. Where Obama can be brought down. Jeff emphasized LaRouche's point about impeachment; we will now take the *Hamiltonian* onto the streets in a heightened way tomorrow morning and Sunday and into next week, to build both this process of veto-override, potential impeachment, Glass-Steagall, and the new Presidency.

Get On Board the New Paradigm Sweeping the Planet

by Kesha Rogers

Sept. 27—The solutions to the prevailing culture of terrorism, war, murder, suicide, and mass killings will only be possible with an end to the prevailing British imperial policy of financial looting and the attendant economic disintegration, which continue to dominate the dying trans-Atlantic system. We must start with the reinstatement of Franklin Roosevelt's original Glass-Steagall Act and a full recovery program based on the advanced science driver and other economic programs proffered by China at the G-20 Summit this month. We now have an obligation to demand that our government re-establish its commitment to the principles defined in the Preamble to our nation's Constitution and our Declaration of Independence—principles that are valid not only for our nation, but universally, for the development of all nations.

How can we tolerate Obama's continued rejection of China's offer of cooperation for economic progress, repeated again by the leadership of China during the G-20 Summit? How can we tolerate Obama's continued promotion of conflicts in the South China Sea, his ongoing policy of regime change in Syria, his aiding and protecting of terrorism, and his protection of Wall Street looting, on behalf the British Empire? The fate and the future of this nation require that we not wait for an already rigged election campaign to act, and rely on its result. No honest solutions can be brought about through the election in November unless Obama is removed now.

Our government must accept the offer China made at the G-20 Summit and join the new paradigm of economic development and cooperation. That is the vehicle by which we can return to our own founding principles. But it will only happen when the people of the United States stop being soft on the murderous policy

en.wikipedia.org

Congress must reject the entire spectrum of Obama's policies in favor of policies that serve the common interests of mankind.

being carried out by President Obama on behalf of the British-Saudi alliance—an alliance for destruction that he has vowed to defend and protect, as emphatically confirmed by his veto of the Justice Against Sponsors of Terrorism Act (JASTA). His veto must be overridden, and we must demand his removal from office now, for the high crimes and indeed the treason that he has committed against this nation.

Before Obama's veto of JASTA, Lyndon LaRouche warned that it was already expected that Obama would veto it, "because he is an agent of the British system." This act of treason against the American people warrants Obama's immediate impeachment.

It is imperative that the American people understand that we are up against a collapsing empire and its financial oligarchy that are out to create total chaos and destruction to put an end to the new paradigm for economic and scientific progress that is already in the process of being created. This empire and its stooge Obama continue to stand in the way, as the very antithesis of economic development and cooperation, but they are vulnerable and can be defeated.

Over the last several weeks, with the G-20 Summit in Hangzhou led by China, followed by the meeting of the UN General Assembly, it has become clear that there are two systems before the world. But only one will prevail. As Helga Zepp-LaRouche made clear in her appeal to the UN General Assembly after the G-20 had met, "The course has been set toward a new financial architecture, and the chance is greater than ever that all nations can participate in the building of the New Silk Road on the basis of win-win cooperation, and that the productivity of the world economy will rise on the basis of innovation, while poverty and the consequences of war are overcome."

Vision of the Hongzhou G-20 Summit

China, joined by Russia and other leading nations throughout the world, continues to stand strong against the geopolitical agenda of global dominance, the agenda of a unipolar world that seeks to keep whole populations of the world backwards and enslaved.

China and the other participants of the G-20 Summit, in their final communiqué, expressed the belief that "Closer partnership and joint action by G-20 members will boost confidence in, foster driving forces for, and intensify cooperation on global economic growth, contributing to shared prosperity and better well-being of the world." The G-20 leaders also state, "We are determined to foster an innovative, invigorated, interconnected and inclusive world economy."

The vision of the Hangzhou G-20 Summit includes the reaffirmation of "our commitment to promote investment with focus on infrastructure in terms of both quantity and quality. We welcome the Joint Declaration of Aspirations on Actions to Support Infrastructure Investment by eleven multilateral development banks, including their announcements of quantitative ambitions for high-quality infrastructure projects within their respective institutional mandates ..."

These eleven multilateral development banks call for up to $1.5 trillion to be invested in infrastructure in the developing world, annually, for the next 15 years. Of this amount, these banks currently commit around $150 billion annually—which in itself is about one-and-a-half times the amount that Obama is spending annually to upgrade the United States' nuclear arsenal to a global first-strike capability. These eleven banks are investing in New Deal style projects, including the building of new and upgraded rail systems, power grids, and advanced agro-industrial projects. There is obviously plenty of room here for U.S. cooperation.

A new paradigm is now sweeping the planet. Our nation and its youth deserve to be a part of such a beautiful future. It is being led by China and Russia, through "development corridor" projects such as the New Silk Road, to which governments representing more than 70 percent of the world's population have made commitments. But Obama not only rejects this beautiful new paradigm in which we have a rightful place: He is determined to halt it as soon as possible—in behalf of his allegiance to an evil empire.

Obama cuts our space program, denying access to scientific progress, while China now leads the charge in defining mankind's extraterrestrial imperative in the development of space, going to the far side of the moon, investing in advanced hypersonic spacecraft, organizing cooperation in space with most of the world for a space station set to be launched by 2020. All this, while Obama is supporting terrorism, promoting conflict and war, and protecting Wall Street's looting of the productive economy, all on behalf of a dying British Empire. Justice will only be served when this evil British-Saudi nexus is ended, Obama is ousted, JASTA is passed, and Glass-Steagall is enacted.

As the World Order Collapses, Solutions Are Needed, Not Propaganda!

by Helga Zepp-LaRouche, chair of the German political party Civil Rights Movement Solidarity (BüSo)

Sept. 24—So many crises in the trans-Atlantic world are coming to a head that it is almost overwhelming: The financial sector faces an imminent new collapse—yet governments remain silent and do nothing. President Obama, with his veto of the Justice Against Sponsors of Terrorism (JASTA) bill, has sided with Saudi Arabia against the victims of the 9/11 attacks, and thus exposed himself to possible impeachment. Tensions between the United States and Europe, and within the European Union (EU), are escalating and reaching the breaking point. The hawks in the United States—with the "unintentional" attack on the Syrian Army at Deir al-Zour and allegations of Russian and Syrian responsibility for the attack on the aid convoy in Aleppo, with no evidence provided—have sought to sabotage the peace efforts by U.S. Secretary of State John Kerry and Russian Foreign Minister Sergey Lavrov, thus risking a major war with Russia.

In the face of these dramatic developments, is there still a chance for a peaceful resolution of these crises?

Yes, there is. But it demands a dramatic turnaround in thinking. European governments and important forces in the United States must take up the concept that China and the other BRICS nations presented in the context of the latest G-20 Summit, in Hangzhou, namely, a win-win mode of cooperation among all nations globally to solve the common problems of mankind: the immediate implementation of a new financial architecture and a reorientation of the world economy on the basis of scientific and technological innovation. In short, the old geopolitical premises must be thrown overboard and the general welfare of all mankind must be taken up as the point of departure for solving each individual crisis.

Most Europeans have absolutely no idea of the level of outrage over Obama's veto of JASTA, the bill passed by both houses of Congress without debate, to permit the relatives of the victims of 9/11 to sue the Saudi government for its support of the terrorists. The families want justice for those they have lost, and see it as a betrayal that Presidents Bush and Obama have covered up this monstrous crime.

Not only did 3,000 people lose their lives then, but now, 15 years after the attack, according to *Newsweek*,[1] approximately 400,000 people—first responders, firemen, policemen, and people who found themselves within a one-and-a-half mile radius of the World Trade Center—are suffering from 70 different varieties of cancer, acute respiratory distress, diseases of the digestive tract, panic attacks and post-traumatic stress disorder, and other illnesses. In short, their lives have been severely impaired or shortened. The overwhelming majority of members of the House of Representatives and the Senate have vowed to override Obama's veto this week. Family members and survivors of the attack have condemned Obama's alignment with the Saudi regime

---

1. "9/11's Second Wave: Cancer and Other Diseases Linked to the 2001 Attacks are Surging," by Leah McGrath Goodman, *Newsweek*, Sept. 7, 2016.

Deir al-Zour, where a U.S.-led strike killed up to 80 Syrian government soldiers.

SOCIETE GENERALE   Deutsche Bank   HSBC

wikimedia   wikimedia

The headquarters of some European Banks towering far too high for the level of their risky assets.

in the harshest terms, and announced an escalation of their campaign for justice.

The Derivatives Risk

Meanwhile, it is common knowledge that the whole trans-Atlantic banking system is on the edge of a new collapse, a systemic crisis which can no longer be papered over with "instruments" like those used in 2008, because these mechanisms—such as quantitative easing, negative interest rates, and helicopter money—are no longer effective.

Thomas Hoenig, vice-president of the Federal Deposit Insurance Corporation (FDIC), released figures on Sept. 20 showing that Deutsche Bank is the riskiest bank in the world. For 42 trillion euros in immediately outstanding derivatives contracts—about three times as much as the total GDP of the Eurozone—it had a leverage ratio (core capital in relation to its total balance sheet) of 2.68% as of June 30. Its ratio of capital reserve to assets (loans) is thus worse than Lehman Brothers' shortly before the 2008 collapse. The FDIC considers outstanding derivatives contracts—a field in which Deutsche Bank is the inglorious world champion—as the greatest systemic risk, against which that bank has virtually no "cushion" in the event of a crisis.

International financial media have noted that the government of Chancellor Angela Merkel is silent about Deutsche Bank's situation, and according to *Bloomberg*, the subject was not even raised at a closed-door session of the Bundestag Finance Committee with Finance Minister Schäuble. But according to the FDIC, something like a dozen more "too big to fail" banks (supposedly too big to be *allowed* to fail) are not in

much better shape. If any one of these banks goes bankrupt, the whole trans-Atlantic financial system will implode, because all of the large and middle-sized banks active in the investment business are greatly undercapitalized.

The $14 billion fine imposed on Deutsche Bank by the U.S. Justice Department for its illegal transactions in the U.S. real estate market between 2005 and 2007 would bring the bank to the point of near ruin, given the mere $19 billion in its capital base: Its stock has fallen from 150 euro a share in 2007 to only 9.35 euro a share on September 15, 2016.

Meanwhile, within the EU, Bundesbank head Jens Weidmann and Italian Prime Minister Matteo Renzi are quarreling over whether the accumulation of bad loans in the Italian banks or the derivatives risk of the banks in Germany are the root of the problem. At the same time, European Central Bank (ECB) head Mario Draghi and German Finance Minister Wolfgang Schäuble are blaming each other for the crisis, the one hammering the negative interest rates of the ECB and the other Germany's austerity policy.

The upcoming October referendum in Italy (which can lead to new elections and an electoral victory for the Eurosceptic Five Star party); the upcoming referendum in Hungry on EU refugee policy; elections in Austria this year, and in France and Germany next year; the collapse of the major political parties and rise of populist to extreme-right parties in several European countries; the huge failure of the EU in the face of the refugee crisis: All of these factors, added to the Brexit and the inability of the European elite to correct its own policies, make the survival of the Eurozone, and of the EU itself, more than doubtful.

Glass-Steagall Now

And what are the governments doing? Instead of acknowledging the failure of their policies, shutting down the banks' casino economy by introducing a Glass-Steagall banking separation system, and finally implementing a policy to defend the general welfare of their peoples—they are redecorating, attempting to present

http://www.gwadarport.gov.pk

The Port of Gwadar, a warm-water, deep-sea port situated on the Arabian Sea in Pakistan, features prominently in the China–Pakistan Economic Corridor plan, and is a crucial link between the ambitious land and sea Silk Road projects.

Areva

Construction of units 5 and 6 of the Fuqing nuclear power plant in April 2015, which will serve as demonstration units for China's new Hualong One reactor design. China National Nuclear Corporation's new reactor design sets the groundwork for China to export its nuclear technology.

gram signed the first Memorandum of Understanding for UN cooperation with China's Silk Road initiative. Li also reported to a forum of sixteen leading UN institutions on China's newly released plan to promote the worldwide realization of the UN Agenda 2030, on Sept. 19. An important component of this plan is the industrialization of Africa and other developing countries, and the establishment of a new financial architecture.

This perspective, which China had already presented at the G-20 Summit, offers an approach to solving the crises before us. Only if the European countries and the United States adopt the solutions implemented in 1933 by Franklin D. Roosevelt for overcoming the financial and economic crisis at that time—solutions implicitly represented today by the Chinese proposals—can an escalation toward a global financial blowout, and from the new Cold War to a thermonuclear world war, be prevented.

A new global Glass-Steagall law must write off the bad debts and derivatives in an orderly fashion. A credit system must be established which exclusively finances investments in innovation and the real economy, doing away with the casino economy based on maximizing profits. The expansion of the New Silk Road into the World Land-Bridge, a program in which more than 70 nations are already participating, is a very concrete option for overcoming geopolitics and putting win-win collaboration for the common aims of mankind on the agenda.

The realization of this perspective, in light of the crises sketched here, may appear to be an unreachable qualitative leap. Only if a sufficient number of forces can bring themselves into a totally new paradigm of thinking, does Mankind have a chance.

new window dressing of their image. On Sept. 16 they bombastically announced a "Bratislava Road Map" and evoked the "spirit of Bratislava," a PR maneuver immediately foiled by Italian Prime Minister Renzi and Hungarian Prime Minister Viktor Orbán, who showed it was all just empty talk.

In contrast, the most important initiative toward a potential solution for these global crises was given impetus by Chinese Prime Minister Li Keqiang at the United Nations General Assembly, now meeting at UN headquarters in New York. Building on the Hangzhou program, Li and the head of the UN Development Pro-

Every Day Counts In Today's Showdown To Save Civilization

II. Stalingrad in Syria?

VIRGINIA STATE SEN. RICHARD BLACK

Letter of Regret to Syria for U.S. Bombing of Soldiers at Deir al-Zour

Sept. 19—Virginia State Senator Richard Black sent the following letter of regret today to the Syrian Ambassador to the United Nations, Hon. Bashar Ja'afari.

I write to express my deepest regrets for the terrible tragedy at Deir al-Zor. The soldiers who were killed and those wounded were among the greatest heroes of the Syrian nation. For years, they defended the city, which was surrounded by ISIS terrorists allied with Turkey, Saudi Arabia, and Qatar. I join the Syrian people in mourning the loss of the soldiers, and I express my sincere condolences to their families.

Courtesy of Sen. Black

President Bashar al Assad (left) meets Virginia State Sen. Richard Black in Damascus, April 28, 2016.

While I cannot say whether this was a deliberate attack, the battle lines at Deir al-Zour have been relatively static for years, and the aircraft attacking their positions were equipped with GPS targeting devices. I am sickened by the possiblity that the attack may have been deliberately launched to support ISIS troops to overwhelm the valiant defenders of the city. I pray that this was not the case.

Normally, I would dismiss the attack as accidental. However, at times the State Department has found ISIS to be a useful tool in the covert U.S. war against Syria. For years, the administration deliberately permitted 2,000 ISIS oil tankers to conduct a massive trade with Turkey to fund the operations of ISIS. It was Russia that finally interdicted the unsavory oil trade with Turkey, forcing ISIS to cut its payroll in half.

Furthermore, my travels beyond Palmyra in April left no doubt that the U.S.-led Coalition deliberately allowed ISIS to cross 100 miles of open desert without dropping a single bomb. They could easily have interdicted the hundreds of tanks and other vehicles that ISIS assembled to seize the city. Clearly, the Coalition hoped that ISIS would fight its way beyond Palmyra and on to the capital of Damascus. They were quite willing to see ISIS impose its gruesome reign of terror on the entire Syrian people. I thank God for those who intervened to prevent this fate from befalling Syria.

I would like to personally apologize for the disgraceful behavior of UN Ambassador Samantha Power when she addressed the United Nations about the incident. I was embarrassed by her callous attitude toward the death and wounding of so many innocent men. Sadly, her attitude is all too characteristric of the bloodthirsty nature of some members of this administration.

I hope that the United States will soon turn the page on its sordid record of employing religious terror to achieve regime change in nations like Libya, Syria, and Yemen. Few Americans realize how deeply complicit our government has become in propagating the wave of terrorism that is engulfing the world today.

I speak for many Americans in asking that you convey my thoughts and prayers to Syria.

Warm regards,
Richard H. Black
Senator of Virginia, 13th District

Obama's Crimes Against Humanity

by Michael Billington

Sept. 24—The film *Snowden*, co-written and directed by Oliver Stone, has been released to the public at a crucial moment in American history. As intended by Stone, the film is having a profound impact on the population, forcing viewers to come to terms with the police state they have lived in since George Bush and Dick Cheney launched the NSA surveillance of every American citizen (with billions of others) in the aftermath of the British-Saudi 9/11/2001 terrorist attack on the United States. And, as the film powerfully demonstrates, Obama, despite his flowery pledges to end this criminal surveillance system, only expanded it further.

The release of Mr. Stone's movie could not have come at a more compelling moment. During the week of the film's premier, Barack Obama vetoed the Justice Against Sponsors of Terrorism Act (JASTA), spitting on the graves of the 3,000 Americans who died in the 9/11 attacks.

Obama's subservience to British and Saudi interests, seen in his refusal to release the "28 pages" for seven years and his veto of JASTA, goes hand in hand with his defense of the NSA surveillance state which is depicted in the film.

At the same period that Obama worked so closely with British interests, Hillary Clinton was complicit in the murder of Libyan President Muammar Qaddafi, and also

A poster for the movie Snowden, *directed by Oliver Stone.*

labeled Edward Snowden a criminal who should "come home and face the music."

The Real Edward Snowden

Despite media characterizations, Edward Snowden was not some mid-level cog or "hacker" in the intelligence community. He was, in fact, a leading creator of many of the surveillance programs from within the CIA and the NSA. He was considered a genius and moved rapidly to extremely high level assignments, designing several of the most sophisticated programs. His job at his last position at a government intelligence center in Hawaii was—in part on his own suggestion—to set up a centralized operation which would compile all the disparate NSA surveillance programs into a single database. It was this centralized program which he would later copy and leak to the world.

Snowden's background, as shown in the film, was as a deeply patriotic individual who wished to serve his country. He personally revolted against what he recognized as a criminal use of these programs during the Bush/Cheney years, but he stuck with the system when Obama, in his campaign speeches in 2008, pledged to end it. Only when it was clear that Obama had lied and was going even further than Bush, did Snowden decide he had to act on his own.

Agence France-Presse reported on Sept. 22 that Oliver Stone, presenting his film at the San Sebastian film festival in Spain's Basque country, said of Obama: "Obama has doubled down on the Bush administration policies. [He] has created … the most massive global security surveillance state that's ever been seen, way beyond East Germany's Stasi [secret police], way beyond that…. Let's beware of fascists and tyrants who tell us 'We are going to protect you.'"

Truth not Propaganda

What Mr. Stone has crafted is not a heavy-handed political propaganda piece. If anything, much of what is presented in the movie is understated. Nothing is explicitly declared to be the truth. Rather, the events of Snowden's life simply unfold, over a period of years, as the realization of what his government is doing becomes increasingly inescapable. And the members of the viewing audience, who have all lived through these events, are presented with the same moral dilemma as Snowden's by the time he decides to act. What makes it even more compelling is that it is all true.

The film is a dramatization, not a documentary, but it was written in cooperation with Edward Snowden personally. It switches seamlessly between dramatization and documentary film clips: President Obama promising to end the illegal surveillance during his 2008 campaign; Hillary Clinton, in a debate, denouncing Snowden as a criminal who "stole very important information that has unfortunately fallen into a lot of the wrong hands," and who must "face the music"; Director of National Intelligence James Clapper telling Sen. Ron Wyden in Senate testimony in 2013 that there were no programs collecting data on millions of Americans (it was this outright lie which Snowden considered the last straw compelling him to act); and even clips of Snowden himself, who is otherwise persuasively portrayed in the film by Joseph Gordon-Levitt.

The film incorporates other aspects of the descent into barbarous criminality under the Bush and Obama administrations. Depictions of drones targetting and destroying human targets identified only by the cell phone being used, with no regard for who else was in the area, are shocking to see.

Although it is not in the film, it is well known that Barack Obama takes great pride in his narcissistic belief that as Emperor, he has the power and the right to compile lists of those he will kill each week through drone strikes, with no concern over due process, nor concern for the "collateral damage." The film does dramatize the well-known story of one drone operator who saw a small child emerge from the house he was targeting, just before the hit, only to be told by his superior not to feel bad, that it was only a dog.

The White House

President Obama and his Secretary of State, Hillary Clinton, in Washington, D.C., May 1, 2009.

Time to Act

Snowden has received very little attention in the major media, and a number of prominent film critics have panned it, but it has been observed that the large audiences that are streaming to see the film leave in a very subdued state, clearly reflecting upon not only the historical drama, but what it says about themselves, for tolerating such vast crimes under Bush and Obama. The unstated question at the end—a question never asked in the film but one which has been placed clearly in the mind of each viewer, is "Who are the real criminals here? Who is it that should be brought to justice?"

In the volatile environment this Autumn in the United States, as Obama stands exposed as a partner of terrorists—in his veto on behalf of Saudi Arabia of the JASTA bill that would allow American victims of the Saudi-funded 9/11 attack on the United States to sue the Saudis in court—the exposure of Obama in the *Snowden* film must add to the moral pressure on all Americans, and citizens of the world, to remove this President from office, and bring him to justice for his crimes against the Constitution and against humanity.

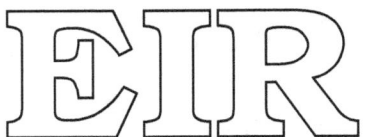

www.ingramcontent.com/pod-product-compliance
Lightning Source LLC
Chambersburg PA
CBHW051953280526
45789CB00009B/3276